The Workers' World at Hagley

THE
WORKERS' WORLD
AT HAGLEY

Glenn Porter

WITH THE ASSISTANCE OF
Jacqueline Hinsley and Joy Kaufmann

HAGLEY MUSEUM AND LIBRARY
WILMINGTON, DELAWARE

To my parents, Pat Paul Porter and Mary Sanders Porter,
and to the memory of my paternal grandfather, Alexander C. Porter,
whose parents came to America from Ireland
in the middle of the nineteenth century.

THIS PUBLICATION WAS MADE POSSIBLE BY A GRANT FROM THE
NATIONAL ENDOWMENT FOR THE HUMANITIES

Designed by Klaus Gemming, New Haven, Connecticut
Composed by Finn Typographic Service, Stamford, Connecticut
Printed by Meriden Gravure Company, Meriden, Connecticut
Reprinted by Stinehour Press, Lunenburg, Vermont

Preface and Acknowledgments

IN RECENT YEARS many historians have turned their attention to the lives and communities of the ordinary men and women of the past. Although such people seldom left the sorts of voluminous personal papers that have helped us understand the elite in American society, scholars have made good use of other kinds of sources, including census and tax records, legal documents, genealogies, and oral histories. *The Workers' World at Hagley* consists mainly of materials drawn from two rich sources that give us the opportunity to see something of the lives of the working families in the Brandywine River communities near the original black powder works of the Du Pont Company. One of those sources is the body of historical photographs now housed in the Hagley Museum and Library. The other is the collection of oral history interviews gathered by the staff of the Hagley Museum from former employees of the powder yards and their families. That project, like the museum itself, was begun in the 1950s. It was carried out largely under the direction of Norman B. Wilkinson, former director of research at the museum, and Joseph P. Monigle, the museum's former deputy director. The interviews and photographs permit us to experience a portion of the lives of the workers and their families.

The part of the workers' world we see in these pictures and remembrances deals only with the last few decades of the history of the powder yards, which were begun in 1802 and closed in 1921. Most of the photographs are from the period of the mid-1880s through about 1910, though it is not always possible to be sure. In many respects, however, the experiences of the workers and their families in that era closely resembled those of earlier generations in the community. Many of the mills, homes, churches, and schools pictured in this book had already been in use for decades when the photos were taken. Many still stand today on the grounds of the Hagley Museum and in the surrounding neighborhood.

We owe what we are able to see and understand of that older world in this publication to many people. A substantial body of research into the history of the community of workers at Hagley was carried out over a period of a quarter century at the Hagley Museum and, in recent years, at the Regional Economic History Research Center. Far more than any other, the work of Harold Hancock has informed and shaped our understanding of this topic. In the latter part of the 1950s Professor Hancock wrote three typescript volumes of excellent research reports for the Hagley Museum on the subject of "The Industrial Worker on the Brandywine." All who have worked on the topic since are immensely in his debt, and I have relied very heavily on Hancock's scholarship.

There are other substantial debts owed to researchers. Several of the scholars who were in residence at Hagley in the late 1970s and early 1980s, including Merritt Roe Smith and Donald R. Adams, Jr., worked on Du Pont materials. Adams's studies of wages, incomes, cost of living, and savings of workers at the Du Pont Company in the nineteenth century have been especially relevant to this publication. A number of the students in my graduate research seminar at the University of Delaware in the fall of 1979 worked on aspects of the workers' lives at Hagley and the adjoining Henry Clay Village area. I am particularly indebted to seminar members Jon Andress, Linda Daur, Dona McDermott, John Rumm, Tim Shickles, William Sisson, Vicky Uminowicz, and Glenn Uminowicz. Scores of other researchers, especially former participants in the Hagley Graduate Program, have contributed essays, reports, and M.A. and Ph.D. theses that have been helpful. Most of these materials are presently stored in the library at Hagley, and I am immensely indebted to Jacqueline Hinsley, former director of research at the museum, for her assistance with those studies, for her generosity in sharing her extensive knowledge of the history of the powder works, and for her unfailing good sense, good humor, and encouragement. Joy Kaufmann, former research assistant at Hagley, helped us with the work of research and the assembling of pictorial and oral history materials. Both Jacqueline Hinsley and Joy Kaufmann participated in the process of choosing the photographs and excerpts from oral history remembrances, and they offered many excellent suggestions about the organization of material.

Others cooperated and assisted in countless ways. Walter J. Heacock, my predecessor as director at Hagley, provided critical support and leadership, not only in conjunction with this publication but also in the implementation of the important changes implicit for the Hagley Museum in the entire exhibit on "The Workers' World." The staff of the Hagley Library, and particularly the Pictorial Collections Department— Dan Muir, Jon Williams, Charles Foote, and George Rineer—were very helpful. Barbara Benson, former editor at Hagley and now executive director at the Historical Society of Delaware, provided counsel and encouragement. David Gilchrist, former director of publications at Hagley, saw the booklet through the production process. Debra Bowers typed the manuscript in her usual excellent fashion.

We are especially grateful for the assistance of the National Endowment for the Humanities and the Andrew W. Mellon Foundation. The Research Grants Division of NEH and the Mellon Foundation have supported the research programs at Hagley in numerous ways since 1977. Funding for this particular publication and for the entire "Workers' World" exhibit came from the Public Programs Division of the National Endowment for the Humanities, and we acknowledge with thanks their generous assistance. We are pleased that the exhibit and this publication represent an opportunity to make research in the humanities available to a wide public audience. We hope that this 1992 reprinting will make this booklet available to an even wider audience than the original 1981 printing.

Glenn Porter
Director
Hagley Museum and Library
1992

THE WORKERS' WORLD AT HAGLEY

In the sweat of thy face shalt thou eat bread, till thou return
unto the ground.

Genesis 3:19

It is as though the world operated on the principle of "truck."
If you want some of this then you must take some of that as well,
even though you do not want it.

David Pye, The Nature of Design, 1964

THIS PUBLICATION came to fruition as part of an exhibit at the Hagley Museum entitled "The Workers' World: The Industrial Village and the Company Town." Like the rest of that exhibit, it represents the joint labors of the staffs of the Museum and of the Regional Economic History Research Center at Hagley. Although the exhibit includes materials on the lives and work of the inhabitants of many industrial villages and company towns, this booklet focuses on a single industrial village – the Brandywine powder-making community founded by Eleuthère Irénée du Pont in 1802.

From the early nineteenth century until the powder yards closed in 1921, that enterprise provided a livelihood for generations of families. Mostly they were immigrants, primarily Irish, but some French, some Italian, and a few others. They lived and worked in a community that lay in the heart of one of the early centers of the American industrial revolution, along the Brandywine Creek in northern Delaware. By the time the yards closed, the small family firm begun in 1802 was well on its way to being the chemi-cal giant the world now knows as E. I. du Pont de Nemours and Company. But that is the story of the company in the twentieth century, and this publication is a part of its story – primarily the experiences of the workers and their families – in the nineteenth century.

The Workers' World exhibit and this publication are intended to give Americans of the 1980s a sense of the lives and work of some of the men, women, and children who participated directly in what we call industrialization. They are not, and do not claim to be, comprehensive. For the most part the focus is on "the workers" rather than the owners and managers of industrial enterprises, though the latter surely worked too. It is impossible to convey any real sense of the lives of the workers and their families without taking into account their relationship with the owners and managers, but the bulk of the exhibit and of this booklet deals with the people who worked directly with the new machines and processes. In this way we hope to respond, in part, to the lament of the descendant of one Hagley workman. "It is such a pity," she said, "that the workingmen have actually been forgotten. All these elaborately furnished homes of the wealthy don't give any indication of how the people lived that did the work."

We cannot, of course, hope to indicate how all the Americans lived "that did the work." A story so large and varied cannot be told fully in a single museum exhibit or a single book. Therefore, the exhibit concentrates on two related settings in which industrialization took place: the industrial village and the company town. This publication provides a closer look at a single manufacturing village, the sort of small industrial community that was relatively isolated and that occupied a semi-rural setting. Because of the central importance of waterpower in the initial stages of industrialization, many of America's mills and factories arose in such settings. The Pennsylvania village described in Anthony Wallace's *Rockdale* was an example of this kind of community, and so were the manufacturing hamlets along the Brandywine Creek in Delaware, including the Du Pont powder operation and the communities that lay adjacent to it. New England was dotted with such places, and they appeared in the Midwest and in the South and elsewhere in America as the nineteenth century passed.

The other, closely related kind of community treated in the exhibit is the company town. A company town was a community dominated by a single firm which was often responsible for planning, creating, and running it. The distinctions between industrial villages, company towns, and other industrial settings are not always precise, but the "ideal types" are reasonably clear. In general, company towns appeared later than in-dustrial villages, and they were usually larger. Sometimes, as in Cohoes, New York, industrial villages evolved into company towns. The earliest example of a company town in America was probably Lowell, Massachusetts; the type spread through northern New England, creating such cities as Lawrence, Massachusetts, and Manchester, New Hampshire, which was dominated by the Amoskeag Company and is described in Tamara Hareven and Randolph Langenbach's book, *Amoskeag: Life and Work in an American Factory-City*. The company town also spread to the South, beginning with Graniteville, South Carolina, at the end of the 1840s and extending into many mill and factory towns of the New South. The company town flourished at the end of the nineteenth century and the early years of the twentieth, reaching perhaps its most comprehensive form in George Pullman's "model town" of Pullman, Illinois, in the early 1880s, a community of more than 8,500 people in 1885 and a direct descendant of Lowell. It was the model for many more such towns, including two that are examined in some detail in the Workers' World exhibit – the Pennsylvania Steel Company complex built in the 1880s and early 1890s at Sparrows Point, Maryland, and the World War I "Westinghouse Village" created by that corporation at Essington, Pennsylvania.

Neither the industrial village nor the company town disappeared abruptly or completely from the American landscape. But changes in the broader economy and society, especially the coming of the automobile, the spread of unions, and the growing involvement of government in the workplace, made for basic alterations in such communities in the twentieth century. Therefore, the exhibit includes materials pertinent to industrial villages and company towns from their beginnings approximately through the era of World War I.

It should perhaps also be emphasized that the exhibit and this publication focus on manufacturing. No significant attention is paid to other forms of work prominent in industrializing America – agriculture, mining, transportation, trade, and so on. Our topic is the work, the homes, and the communities of laboring people directly involved in the manufacture of goods.

For a variety of reasons, the nature of the relations between labor and capital in industrial villages and company towns was somewhat different from that in the cities. One important difference was that there was considerably less *open* conflict associated with industrialization in the kind of places examined in the exhibit. There were, of course, exceptions to this pattern, including the well-known strikes and violence that marked the company towns of Pullman, Illinois, and Homestead, Pennsylvania, during the depression of the 1890s. But the generalization still seems sound.

In the case of the Hagley powder-making community, there was clearly a much greater tendency toward outward calm and much less open industrial conflict than there was in the nearby city of Wilmington. The first real strike at Hagley, for example, did not occur until 1906, after more than a century of operation. At other industrial villages along the Brandywine the story was much the same. In urban Wilmington there was always a stronger tradition of worker organization, of strikes, and of demands for changes such as shorter working hours. The city's workers – particularly the more skilled ones, such as coopers, cordwainers, carpenters, and machinists – apparently found it both easier and more necessary to organize and to fight for change than did the workers in the semi-rural villages up the Brandywine. As industrialization progressed, however, there was a general trend toward more frequent and more open tension and conflict between manufacturers and workers in industrial villages, in company towns, and in cities.

Neither the conflict nor the calm indicates the full complexity and ambiguity of experiences in the workers' world. There are two stereotypes that most present-day Americans have of our industrial experience in the past. One is the "workers' paradise" view, in which honest, industrious workers sought "progress," achieved it readily, and found the streets virtually paved with gold. The other, and perhaps more widespread, stereotype is that of the abused, downtrodden, and helpless worker immiserated by capitalism and immortalized in the superb photographs produced by Lewis Hine at one stage of his career. Difficult though it is, we need to try to understand the workers' world as one of mixed blessings, of both good and bad. Neither stereotype is truly accurate.

One of the clearest "good" elements was that industrialization meant material progress. Looking at the economy as a whole and in long-term perspective, it is clear that the material lot of the average worker got better and better from 1800 to 1920. The income and wealth of most workers rose considerably over time; there is no doubt that the material well-being of most individuals improved during their lifetimes. Similarly, it is clear that things were better economically for most American workers than for their counterparts in other countries, and that was important to a nation of immigrants. As historians David and Sheila Rothman have noted, "The satisfaction of living better than they had before may well have helped wed American workers to the industrial system... many of the workers were immigrants... these people were in fact substantially better off in this country. The American dream... was not all myth." Further, wages and incomes of workers in manufacturing were higher than those of farm laborers and those of most other working-class groups. Economically, the industrial world represented progress for most, whether compared to the past, to conditions prevailing elsewhere in the world, or to other ready job possibilities in America.

For most of the workers at Hagley, material progress was a reality. Most were immigrants, and industrial work on the Brandywine meant the opportunity to enjoy a better life and higher levels of living. Primarily because manufacturing, unlike agriculture, offered virtually year-round work, laborers could earn much larger incomes than they could on the farm. Donald Adams's studies of the wages, incomes, cost of living, and savings of workers at Hagley up to the Civil War clearly show a general pattern of material betterment. In the long run, throughout the process of industrialization the workers' wages and incomes rose, though there were what Adams terms "periodic but temporary setbacks." As the nineteenth century passed, working-class families in manufacturing had more money to spend on things other than the necessities of life. At Hagley, many

workers were able to save substantial portions of their incomes, and they had a strong incentive to do so, because the Du Pont Company paid 6 percent interest on balances in excess of $100 that were left with the firm, an unusual arrangement in manufacturing. Adams's conclusion is very likely correct for the entire period that the powder yards were in operation: "In terms of real earnings, the industrial workers of the Brandywine region appear to have kept pace and shared fully in the benefits" of American economic growth.

Although that was the experience for most workers, both on the Brandywine and elsewhere, that is not the whole story. Some workers always lived on the edge of subsistence, and the danger of injury, layoffs, and unemployment was a constant threat to the progress of any individual or family. And, if one thinks of poverty as a relative rather than an absolute condition, many workers lived in poverty simply because they had less than those at the top of the social system. The distribution of wealth and of income was always very uneven throughout the period from 1800 to 1920, as it still is today. The average worker did accumulate material wealth during a lifetime, but it was relatively rare for working-class people to move to middle-class or upper-class occupations or to become rich. That *did* happen, and it happened often enough to keep many people believing in "social mobility," but the odds were against its happening to any particular individual.

Whether they were moving up or down or just getting along, most working families in industrial villages and company towns received some benefits in addition to wages. In varying degrees these included such things as free or subsidized housing, death benefits, medical care, schools, recreational facilities, churches, and the like. The motives of employers in providing or supporting these were mixed. In many cases there was a genuine wish to improve workers' conditions and a real concern for the welfare of the work force. In addition, there were other, nonaltruistic motives, such as the need to attract and hold a work force and to improve productivity by eliciting goodwill on the part of the workers. Furthermore, the provision of such services made employees more dependent on their bosses and permitted more extensive social controls to be exercised over them. The threat of eviction or withdrawal of other benefits discouraged workers from "making trouble." Many of the aspects of community life that were provided or supported by employers enabled them to influence the behavior of workers. Local churches often conveyed messages of stability and conservatism, as did schools. When the Delaware legislature issued a charter to the new Brandywine Manufacturers' Sunday School in 1817, for example, it stated that "the establishment of Sunday Schools, especially in the vicinity of extensive manufactories, is calculated, not only to promote the instruction of youth, in those useful establishments, in the rudiments of learning, but to conduce greatly to their good and orderly behavior." The records of that nondenominational school show that "attentive," "quiet," and industrious behavior was praised, while idleness was attacked. After the spread of public schools, American schoolchildren were frequently given rewards for "good" behavior, including small cards bearing such messages as "Learn

to Wait." Similarly, employers often sought to keep saloons out of their communities in order to encourage sobriety and industriousness and to combat what they saw as laziness and drunkenness.

In its extreme forms, such as in Pullman and Cohoes, company paternalism "followed the working class family from factory to home to leisure activities and moral education," wrote historian Daniel Walkowitz. "Within this semi-controlled environment the manufactuer sought to instruct his work force in the 'moral' discipline which would reinforce factory work discipline." As nineteenth-century economist Richard Ely said of Pullman, "The citizen is surrounded by constant restraint and restrictions, and everything is done for him, nothing by him." In a material sense workers in such environments often were relatively well off, but a price was paid in terms of social control. Economic historian Edward Kirkland once argued that "whether paternalism is good or bad is a matter of definition. If by it is meant a sense of obligation for the welfare of workers or even a spirit of *noblesse oblige,* paternalism would seem more commendable than harmful; if company town paternalism involved interference in the private lives of the inhabitants or gave the employer an immense advantage in his controversies with the workers, the judgment might well be different." In most cases paternalism involved both the positive and the negative aspects mentioned by Kirkland.

Certainly that was true at Hagley. The relatively good income and savings of many workers have already been discussed, and those material rewards were buttressed with others. The du Ponts appear to have had a genuine concern for their loyal workers and a sense of obligation toward them. In many respects this was manifested in a fashion similar to that in other industrial villages – the provision of inexpensive or free housing, of gardens that workers' families could use to supplement their incomes, of gifts on holidays, of occasional outings, of support for churches and schools for the working class. In some ways the benefits for powder workers were greater than was common: the payment of interest on accounts left with the company; the provision of medical services either free or at low cost, which was rare indeed in nineteenth-century manufacturing; and an unusual program of pensions and other assistance for widows and families of powder workers killed in the explosions that periodically rocked the yards. To some extent this assistance can be attributed to the unusually dangerous nature of work "in the powder," as the workers called it. Industrial work was generally perilous, but work in an explosives manufactory was particularly so, and this made it in the company's own interest to try harder than others to retain its work force by increasing the benefits. But the assistance that was extended to workers at Hagley also rested in the du Ponts' real sense of *noblesse oblige,* a sense of obligation to loyal and productive workers. In many instances the Du Pont Company provided help to those deemed deserving, such as assisting in the immigration of relatives and friends of workers, and helping those rare employees who could afford to buy their own farms or houses to get good titles when they retired or moved on. In 1843, for example, Alfred du Pont personally saw to the securing of a good land title for a worker, explaining, "I am bound to protect the interests of the people in my employment." Because all these benefits could be taken away from troublesome employees at the discretion of the employer, they also served as one of the elements that gave employers great power over the workers. The paternalistic impulse, resting in part on self-interest and in part on a sense of moral obligation, brought with it to the workers at Hagley the same mixture of material benefits and enhanced employer control that it brought everywhere else in industrial America.

As we have already seen, this combination of relatively good material rewards for workers and the relatively greater power of manufacturers in the often isolated industrial villages and company towns made such environments less prone to outward, overt conflict between workers and managers than was the case in large industrial cities. This appears to have been true in Europe as well as America. In their study of *Strikes in France, 1830-1968,* for example, Edward Shorter and Charles Tilly found that the level of strikes was in direct proportion to the extent of what they called the "associational foundation" (unions and other associations both formal and informal) among workers. Further, they found that larger cities, which usually had several industries and a range of employment opportunities, made available many more "associational possibilities," thereby making interaction, cooperation, and collective action by the workers likelier. This was much less true of single-industry villages or towns. The same phenomenon was noticed by Daniel Walkowitz in his comparative study of the neighboring New York communities of Troy and Cohoes, significantly entitled *Worker City, Company Town.*

Troy offered much more in the way of associational possibilities and industrial conflict than did the company town of Cohoes.

Even in the industrial village and the company town, however, tension and conflict appeared between workers and management. Sometimes this manifested itself in the form of drinking on the job, absenteeism, lower production levels than the workers were capable of, and minor pilferage of company-owned goods. Occasionally it meant open clashes, in the form of strikes, violence, and destruction of property. As the scale and corresponding impersonality of labor-management relations grew in the latter part of the nineteenth century, these conflicts became more frequent. When open clashes did erupt they came most often in times of general depression, such as the 1870s and the 1890s. They also came when the economic fortunes of an individual industry or firm turned down due to shifting markets, tighter competition, and the like. Such situations sometimes led management to cut wages or to lay off workers, and that made more difficult the preservation of the customary quiet relations between bosses and workers. Paternalism meant obligations on both sides, including a responsibility for managers to make on occasion some sacrifice for the workers' benefit, such as keeping factories open even during slack times. In part, to do so was simply enlightened self-interest on the part of firms anxious not to lose their work forces. But it was also a part of the unarticulated set of assumptions and expectations that often convinced workers and owners that they had a mutuality of interests.

In Pullman, for example, the famous strike broke out during the depression year of 1894, fourteen years after the town began. Matters exploded when the workers came to feel that the company no longer had their interests, as well as its own, at heart. Although it was still making good money on operations elsewhere, it was not doing so on the car manufacturing works at Pullman in the bad times that followed the Panic of 1893. At the town of Pullman the firm cut wages and began layoffs, but it kept rentals on company housing at the old rates. The workers came to feel frustrated, trapped, and abused because it seemed to them that they were being asked to bear all the burden of hard times. A local Methodist clergyman summed up the workers' sense of the mutual obligations under paternalism: "They started," he said, "on the basis that their system is paternalistic... founded upon a desire to improve the workingmen and to solve the industrial situation... on the basis of a mutual recognition. Now... the Pullman company... ought not at least to cut them so severely, but share up with them, from the standpoint that it is a paternalistic system." The company, of course, felt that it *was* "sharing up" with its employees by keeping the works open on a reduced basis, even though it might well have liked to shut them down entirely until orders picked up. Hard times, for a single worker, a single industry, or for the whole economy, put great pressures on the system of mutual obligations and benefits that usually bound workers and managers together in a surface calm.

Other stresses came from the interrelated factors of technological change and the growing scale of manufacturing business. For a variety of reasons — the press of competition, the wish to improve output and quality, the wish to replace unruly but skilled workers — American business introduced new manufacturing technologies, new machines and processes, throughout the 1800-1920 period. This technical and economic progress lay at the heart of the long-run prosperity enjoyed and celebrated by the great majority of Americans, owners, managers, and workers alike. If technical progress is considered in individual situations, however, it again manifests the complexities and ambiguities that marked industrialization as a whole. The introduction of a new machine often threatened the local workers by embodying and replacing part or all of the skills that made them scarce and valuable labor. It also often made it possible for fewer workers to turn out more goods, which again threatened the labor force that was faced with the new technology. In addition, over time the capabilities of the machines tended to define the pace and the nature of work, resulting in a loss of workers' control over the basic nature of their jobs.

In a culture that valued material progress and rising productivity so highly, it was very difficult for workers to admit, even to themselves, that some of their feelings amounted to an opposition to economic progress. In America there was much less of that opposition than in Europe, and it was most strongly evident in the United States in cases where new technologies supplanted older artisan methods of production. Few American workers opposed "progress" in the abstract. But in any individual case that progress often meant a decline in the workers' control of the job, in their power, and in the employment opportunities for those who had been producing with the old technology.

Of course, viewed as a whole, the process of technological advance and economic growth also produced vast new employment possibilities. This is the essence of what economist Joseph Schumpeter called "creative destruction," the replacing of old industries and methods with new ones. To the economist this is a good thing because it represents increased productivity and leads labor to move to the job opportunities that bring the greatest returns: it is efficient for the system as a whole. To the individual laborers, it was often a bad thing because it reduced their power, intensified the pace of work, threatened their jobs, and sometimes forced them to go elsewhere in search of other work.

Technical progress also contributed mightily to the creation of larger and larger productive units. Labor forces grew at individual mills or plants, and eventually many firms became large enough to include several factories. This made it increasingly hard to maintain the older, more personal style of labor-management relations in which owner-managers knew their workers as individuals. Bureaucracy and system came to replace old methods in terms of planning and routing jobs within the factory, controlling materials and tools, combating absenteeism and tardiness, and in defining the nature of work within the factory. The rise of "scientific management" and the creation of personnel departments in large companies were managerial efforts to improve efficiency, but one of their results was that relationships between workers and managers grew more impersonal and mechanical. Labor leader Samuel Gompers spoke for many workers when he complained that "the employees are

Pierre Gentieu, 1842-1930

not known as men at all but are known as numbers."

On the Brandywine, too, the tensions that were often associated with the growing scale of industrial operations were apparent. The size of the powder-making operation of the Du Pont Company grew in the nineteenth century; the yards steadily occupied more ground, and many buildings that had begun as other industrial sites, such as textile mills, were incorporated into the Du Pont powder plant. More importantly, the company expanded in the decades after the Civil War to include many other factories and sites in addition to the Brandywine powder yards that had given it birth. "By 1894," wrote Harold Hancock, "E. I. du Pont de Nemours and Company owned seventeen complete manufactories" in Delaware, Pennsylvania, Tennessee, and Iowa. Inevitably, the increase in size brought with it a more complex managerial organization. Although most of the du Ponts remained near the birthplace of their family's enterprise, the old black powder yards grew less and less important in the overall scheme of company operations. The death in 1889 of General Henry du Pont, the head of the firm and the family, marked a shift in the older, close paternalistic relationships between the Hagley workers and the owners of the business. More impersonal and more efficient management techniques were introduced, causing some brief conflicts with a minority of disgruntled employees in the form of a wave of barn burnings and destruction of du Pont property. The trend toward larger scale, more impersonal, and more modern management and organization accelerated even more after 1900 as the Du Pont Company was transformed into a modern corporation. By the time the powder yards closed in 1921, they and the way of life they represented had both become something of an anachronism.

We see glimpses of that way of life in the material that follows. The historical photographs give a tangible sense of the workers' world in the Brandywine Valley at Hagley and nearby Henry Clay Village. Many of the photographs were the work of Pierre Gentieu (1842-1930), a French immigrant worker who rose to a modest management position in the powder yards. Writing, drawing, and photography were his avocations, and it is to him that we owe much of the pictorial record of the workplaces, community institutions, and people of the powder yards in the final decades of black powder manufacture on the Brandywine.

The photographs of Pierre Gentieu and others come even more alive in company with the recollections of former workers and their families. Together they give us a look at the turn-of-the-century Brandywine Valley and at many of the people who lived, worked, and died in it. Their way of life was very different from ours. Home, work, and community were all closely tied together. The "little towns" of worker hamlets and the stores, churches, schools, and saloons were permeated by the sounds of the mill bells and the mills themselves; periodically they were shaken with the sounds of the dreadful explosions that threatened every minute of their lives. Residents shared their experiences in a small-town, almost rural closeness that brought people together and at the same time stifled individuality. It was, of course, a community and time when women's roles were more restricted and more narrowly defined than they are today. Women played vital parts in the life of the industrial village – earning wages mostly in textile mills or as domestic servants, or performing the critical economic roles of taking care of paying boarders, sewing, laundering, cooking, canning, gardening, rearing children, and sometimes earning money peeling the willows used in the charcoal making that was essential to black powder manufacture. Like most working-class communities of the day, the central events of life were those associated with births, deaths, and marriages. Churches played an important part, particularly for the women, who were excluded from so many activities in society. Politics seems to have been about as important, or unimportant, to people then as it is today. Entertainment was simple, and the community passed most days with little contact with the outside world.

It was neither the good old days nor the bad old days. It was simply different. People neither rejoiced in their freedom from commuting, crime, and big government nor suffered from the lack of television, paid vacations, and automobiles. All that lay ahead. But their world was changing, and the time was not far away when change would cause the powder yards, the economic heart of the community, to shut down. The people who lived there would go on, some to other jobs and some to distant places, just as the company itself had done.

Their way of life, the workers' world of the industrial village, however, did not disappear completely. Some of its old paternal traditions were reshaped and persisted in new, corporate forms. Most importantly, in the photographs, in the memories of the participants and their families, and in the physical setting of the Hagley Museum and its neighborhood, they live on.

It is pretty through here. I used to go down through that bridge on a moonlit night in November and look up the creek, and it was beautiful.

There were some little towns here: Squirrel Run, Henry Clay, Upper Banks and Charles's Banks, and Wagoner's Row. Twenty-seven houses were right up there in the back of Walker's Mill.

All my life I was around the powder yards. I played around the yards and fished in that creek many times. You could drink that water if you wanted to.

They used to call that the "Poor Man's Beach."

People had cows, and most of the people used the right-hand side of the bridge going over and coming back, but these old cows would get in there in the summertime and lay down at night, and, by gosh, you'd come over there and stumble over a darned old cow. That's true. Saturday night the people would get drunk around here. Oh, it was terrible. The saloons would close up.

They didn't bother much with what was going on in the rest of the world.

We had no jail or nothing like that. We didn't even know what a policeman looked like.

*Many a day I put in skating. The ice used to be eight and
ten inches thick. We found the best skating right down here.*

*When the creek froze, people skated on the Brandywine,
but always outside the Yards.*

Tom Toy had a saloon there along the Creek road. He had two bars on Sunday.
He had a Catholic and a Protestant bar. I was never in there, to tell you the
truth. That was ahead of my time. Anyhow, when St. Joseph's Mass was over
they'd come down there – and when Green Hill Presbyterian Church [was
over]. It was about equally divided, about half Catholics and half Protestants
worked in the Yards at that time . . . northern Irish, they'd fight and raise
the devil – beat one another.

There was never very much contention among them. Maybe on pay nights
they'd go down and have a little fun and have a little bat around town.

Bob Blakely had a store in Squirrel Run. Sam Frizzell's was right this side of Breck's Lane, and Harry Gregg had a store there at the bottom of Rising Sun Lane. Billy Hunter had the old Stirling Store at Wagoner's Row.

The men were Democratic or Republican. They used to have all the elections at the Mt. Pleasant Saloon, up there.

There was a tavern up at the corner at St. Joseph's Church. There were a lot of taverns along the creek. The Black Cat and Blakely's. There were clubs – the Hibernians were the Irishmen, and the Italians had their own.

They had a Republican [Club] here, and they used to call it Tippecanoe.

They had what they called a Businessman's Parade when McKinley was running for president. They went around to every man to get him to turn out in the parade. They told him it wasn't political, it was business. They were working for McKinley. And this Francis G. du Pont was the man who went around and asked them to go out. And I know lots of men went out in that parade because he asked them but didn't vote for McKinley. As they went along, people would say, "Hey, you son-of-a-bitch, you turned out for your job."

Before the trolley line was built, people used to come out to Rising Sun Hill and walk down to go to work if they didn't live here.

Sunday was observed very well.
They rested. Of course, they
had been working six days.

We had very little social life, except what we had at church.

We knew everybody over there because we went back and forth across that field to Sunday school, and people that lived there, we knew all those people.

We all attended Alexis I. [du Pont School].

I went to the Yellow School up at Barley Mill Lane and Montchanin Road. There were four grades and two teachers. There was quite a few teachers over the years. There was Sally Pickles, and Mamie Withers, and Bess Stirling, the daughter of Victor Stirling, the store man.

Most of them stopped after the fourth grade. The girls stayed home and did housework and that kind of stuff.

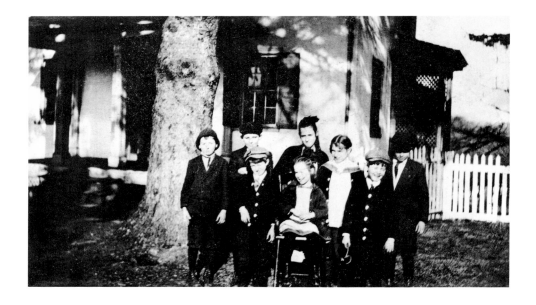

We used to play "Run, Sheepie, Run," where you kept on the move all the time, and they'd try to catch you. Then there was a game called "Hunt the Hare." You used to hide in that game, sort of like hide-and-seek.

When we took a bath, that was maybe once a week or maybe once every two weeks. Of course, in the wintertime, you didn't take one quite so often.

We used to have square dances at Breck's Mill and up at the Du Pont Club. They had a club for the workingmen up there. Had a nice club up there. We used to have a wonderful time.

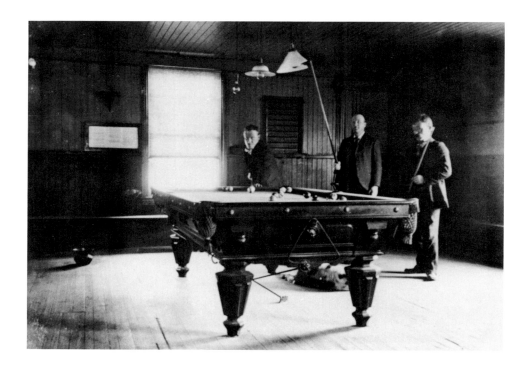

*If they wanted to have a dance they would swing in
your own house and kick up a party. Breck's Mill
was used for a lot of dances, balls, and parties.*

When the barley mill burned the piles of wheat burned there for six weeks afterward, just smoldering. They'd throw water on it, but finally they left it go.

I think it was a Saturday that Rokeby [Mill] burned.

The men really loved Mr. Alfred I. [du Pont]. When my father died
he sent a great big wreath of flowers. He always had parties for us in
Breck's Mill every Christmas. Mr. Alfred I. was very fond of music. He
would play Santa Claus, and he would give us all a box of candy and also
a toy, and refreshments would be served, and we'd have a good time.
After you passed fourteen you didn't get invited, but some of those kids
on the Brandywine never got older than fourteen.

He took over Breck's Mill, which wasn't used any more by the company,
for the orchestra, and also for the entertainment of the boys and girls
of the community. Every Christmas we were invited there, and we all
filed by Mr. du Pont and the wife and children and were presented with
gifts. Mr. du Pont also invited us to come to his house, "Swamp Hall,"
on Halloween night. He always had a large bag of dimes and nickels,
and he threw them up in the air and watched us scramble for them.

*The du Ponts were so nice to us. We had no fear of any du Pont.
We did respect them very much; it was like seeing the President of the
United States or the King of England when any of them came along.
It was always "Mr. Alfred," or "Mr. Frank," or "Mr. Henry," or "Mr.
Eugene," and "Miss Louise" and "Miss Joanna."*

*We would speak, but there was always that class distinction there.
You were workers on the place, and there was a difference.*

*He'd tell you what to do. He'd send you there. He'd do that
because he was monarch of all he surveyed.*

First came the French, and then came the Irish, and then came the Italians.

I'm of Irish descent. My daddy was born in Ireland. My mother was born and raised on the Brandywine, in the same house where I was born, but it's torn down now.

It took him seventy-three days to come here from Ireland. He came in a sailboat. He left Ireland when he was seventeen. The first place he worked was Du Pont's. He had a cousin who worked here. His name was also Campbell. He came here first, and then he sent for my father. He was from the same part of Ireland.

They didn't have much luggage or baggage. I still have my father's tin box, and it isn't very big. It's marked "Steerage," so I guess that's the way he came.

Several of our relatives came over here and lived at our house until the du Ponts had a place for them in the Yard, or the girls were given positions in the du Ponts' homes. They liked to get girls from Ireland for maids.

This wood-grained tin trunk was brought from Ireland by Edward Beacom, who came to work in the powder yards in 1870. (Hagley Museum)

I'll tell you what the houses were like. Just four walls, no conveniences.
They were comfortable. They had the privies in the backyard – and
they were good substantial houses, good and warm.

A lot of them had fireplaces in them, and then they got stoves, what they
used to call "parlor" stoves. And the cookstoves in the wintertime,
they did the cooking.

I know we loved that little house. Everyone had flower boxes in the front. Squirrel Run was so clean. Right across the street from our house there was a little shed. Then outside beside the shed was the coal box for our stove. My mother baked many a loaf of bread in that stove. We had the living room and the kitchen downstairs. Then there was two bedrooms upstairs. We had plenty of room even though we had all those children.

My father was the first one of our family to come to Squirrel Run about the 1870s. My mother came in 1881, but she wouldn't go back because she had such a rough voyage.

My father came from County Fermanagh, North Ireland, and my mother came from County Armagh.

Some had gardens there as you go up Blacksmith Shop Hill. That was all gardens there. The blacksmith shop was there at the gate.

There was this great big living room and then what we called the pantry; and the stairway, which was a crooked one, went up out of the pantry. Then on the other side of that there was a great big kitchen which was only one story. My mother had a kitchen stove, a settee and a big sideboard, about eight or ten chairs, and a bench table. We ate off the table, and our schoolbooks were kept on the seat underneath. Then we had a pair of steps go up the hill in back, and we had a chicken shed.

Everybody in our house had a chore. Usually mine was cleaning. Then you had the dishes and beds to make. That's what amazes me today, just amazes me, to think of the children not having anything to do. My mother found things for you to do. And then when the canning season was on, you always had to help with that.

She generally bought on a large scale. She'd bake her own bread, and this sounds like exaggeration but it's the truth, she'd bake fifty-two loaves of bread a week.

We lived in a house in Walker's Banks. My father, on account of being a powderman, didn't have to pay no rent. Anybody who worked in the powder mills didn't pay. Then later on, I think they charged.

Everybody lived out there worked or did something
for the Company or the Yard. Or they didn't live there.

We had potatoes and string beans and beets and cabbage and lettuce and tomatoes, and they put in enough potatoes to do them for the winter.

Every Fourth of July we'd have our first potatoes. We did all the preparing of the garden by hand.

We had chickens and a garden. I used to deal in rabbit dogs.

All through here used to be open country. Some had two or three rabbit dogs, foxhounds. Oh, we had a good time.

Right across from the dam was Chicken Alley.

They had carpenters, to maintain the houses, but if the occupant wanted to paint a door or a shed, or something like that, he'd go get the paint at the [company] Paint Shop. They supplied materials and you did some of the work.

In those days they raised such large families, they worked and came home from work and walked around and talked to their neighbors, and went to bed because they had to get up early in the morning.

My niece Elsie said she thought the world was coming to an end
that day. She finally got underneath the dining room table.
It damaged the houses so that they moved some of the families out.

Bell used to ring about five minutes to seven in the morning and five minutes to one in the middle of the day. Just enough time for them to get their overalls on and blouse. Start right on the dot.

He asked me why I wanted to come here and I told him I was young and I could grow up with the business, and you have steady work here.

Once they did try to form a labor union. I don't know about the feeling of the men. I never bothered with it. I stayed away from the yard until they got it settled. There was no serious trouble. That was the only time. It was for about a month. I can't tell you just when it was — close to 1900.

When my father began he worked on General Henry [du Pont's] farm. He went from the farm to the composition house, and then he went from there to yard foreman. Yard foreman had charge of building roads, shoveling snow, keeping up the track, etc. After being foreman about thirty years he was pensioned off.

My father-in-law was watchman in that place. He used to be boss carpenter and he got his arm blew off by the cannon up here at a celebration of the Fourth of July. So they put him in here "watching."

My granddaddy was killed there in 1861. My grandmother got a widow's pension — $8.00 a month and a free house — and the right to keep boarders.

Some of them would go toward Long Row and we wouldn't see them leave but the others crawling up from the yard — tired out from working hard. Yet I think most of the workmen were satisfied with their jobs.

Worker's dinner pail, tinned steel, ca. 1890. (Hagley Museum)

They'd say, "Here comes the powder monkey." Every month,
you know, we would go into town. Get paid every month.
Walk up to the top of Rising Sun Hill.

Many people thought working here was worth the money, but they were scared to work in the powder – outside of the Italians and the Irish. There was something fascinating about it, though.

They would ring it for lunch. They didn't ring it at quitting time – not that I know of. Morning, then at noon. I never heard tell of them ringing at quitting. The people knew when it was time to quit.

It was six days, ten hours a day. Worked nine hours on Saturday. We got paid for sixty hours a week. All hours were the same except we had no light in wintertime and had to quit when it got dark. They had candles we could work by if we had something in particular.

*I just forget what year that was, but they had a strike here,
and, of course, these Irish, they wouldn't give in and the
company wouldn't give in. Of course, the company didn't
have to because they had too many others – they could just let
them sit. They let them sit I guess for three or four months.*

*They simply decided to strike. Mr. Lammot du Pont told
them, "Nothing doing." And the thing went off and they never
had a bit of trouble after that.*

Mr. Frank du Pont — his son fired a man in the black powder for doing something there. He asked him what he fired him for and he told him. Well, he asked him, "Don't you know that man has a family? He has a family to support. Now you take him back again." And it was done.

[My father's] duties was at night and he had to patrol the Yard after this big explosion. And he was going through the Yard about 2:00. Somebody put their hand on his shoulder, and it was Mr. Frank du Pont. He said, "I just came to see if you were on the job." Father said he knows his hair turned white. He said he was really scared.

There was no notion of unionism in my day. Never heard tell of it. All a sociable crowd and everybody seemed to be satisfied. You met every man somewhere. He either lived in that section or going to work or something. You had fun everywhere you went. All the people knew each other. Give you a hand at anything. Almost everyone lived around here in my day. They all footed it to work.

I considered anything dangerous where powder was.

I was a mile and a half from the Yard. When we heard the explosion we were let out of school, and we ran to the Upper Yard to see it. The houses were all demolished. I saw a lady out on the roof of a house on a "bed tick," we called them. She was dying. Her name was Rose Ann Dougherty. She had a boardinghouse there. Her husband had been killed in the powder [mills] years before.

I'll never forget the scenes I witnessed from our house right after an explosion. They used to flock down – the people from Free Park used to flock down past our house. It was just terrible! You would hear these Irish women calling out, "Worra, worra, where's my John?" Just ring in your ears for weeks afterward. And they would come up and you could tell by the way that woman was supported by another woman that that woman's husband was gone.

There was a good many boys worked in the keg factory, you know. You had to be a pretty quick worker around them machines. About once every two weeks a boy would get his finger off if he didn't watch himself. Right here in the Keg Mill.

Little boys got their fingers smashed up in the tin shop here. Dr. Greenleaf, he was the du Pont family physician and also the surgeon. He would take them little boys in the summertime right out on the porch. He'd get a good strong man around the neighborhood. He'd put his instruments there, and he would take them little boys' fingers off and dress them and there would be no ether or nothing. Those poor little boys were howling and screaming. I saw that. You know that was terrible. They didn't know anything about hospitals.

   We used to have fun, though. Everybody was happy and we walked a lot.

The first thing he told me, "First of all, you know, when you're in an office you keep your mouth shut."

I said, "I'm well aware of that, Mr. du Pont. That's been a Brandywine characteristic. Keep your mouth shut. Don't hear anything. Don't see anything, or don't talk."

He says, "That's it."

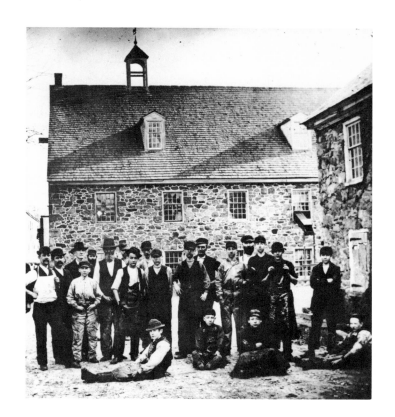

The blacksmith shop [was] where we children spent hours, watching the blacksmith or his assistant fashioning objects on the anvil for use in the mills.

The wagons were built by the company. Most of them, I guess, would have been [built] up at the old wheelwright shop in the middle of the Yard. Most of them were painted green with red wheels. Some of them were covered.

Photograph captions

All photographs are from the collections of the Hagley Museum and Library.

They knew that their life depended on this being careful. If you were working in the mill with me I watched you. I wasn't afraid myself but I was afraid that the other fellow might do something.

I was working with my old man in Walker's Mill when the explosion happened. The first thing I saw was the weather coming in. Coming right down in. All the windows blew out all along on one side of the mill there. One right after the other.

I still have a very good memory of the men, after there would be an explosion, the men going around with these buckets with a red handkerchief over it and picking up the pieces of the men, you know.

There were no vacations then. They never got a vacation
only when they were sick. Six days a week.

There were five of us and my grandmother lived with us all, either my grandmother
or my aunt lived with us all the time, and we usually had two boarders because my father
didn't make enough money to support the whole family and so of course my mother
fed the boarders. And then in harvest time she had to feed the harvesters. Just lunch,
but a lunch was a dinner.